Super Goofy Jokes

by
Jacqueline Horsfall

Illustrated by
Rob Collinet

STERLING PUBLISHING CO., INC.
New York

For Dylan

Library of Congress Cataloging-in-Publication Data

Horsfall, Jacqueline.
  Super goofy jokes / Jacqueline Horsfall ; illustrated by Rob Collinet.

    p. cm.
  Includes index.
  ISBN 1-4027-0927-7
  1. Wit and humor, Juvenile. [1. Jokes.] I. Collinet, Rob, ill. II.
Title.
PN6166 .H69 2004
818'.602--dc22

                                    2003024417

10 9 8 7 6 5 4 3 2 1

Published by Sterling Publishing Co., Inc.
387 Park Avenue South, New York, NY 10016
Text © 2004 by Jacqueline Horsfall
Illustrations © 2004 by Rob Collinet
Distributed in Canada by Sterling Publishing
C/o Canadian Manda Group, One Atlantic Avenue, Suite 105
Toronto, Ontario, Canada M6K 3E7
Distributed in Great Britain and Europe by Chris Lloyd at Orca Book
Services, Stanley House, Fleets Lane, Poole BH15 3AJ, England
Distributed in Australia by Capricorn Link (Australia) Pty. Ltd.,
P.O. Box 704, Windsor, NSW 2756, Australia

Contents

1. Nature Noodles

Where do worms get their mail?
   At the compost office.

What would you get if worms ruled the earth?
   Global worming.

Why do lightning bugs get A's in school?
   They're very bright.

What do frogs think of flies?
   They're toadally awesome.

How do lobsters get to the airport?
By taxi crab.

Where do little elm trees go after kindergarten?
Elm-mentary school.

What kind of nuts don't grow on trees?
Donuts.

What does an ash tree take for a headache?
Ash-pirin.

What do ferns do when winter comes?
Turn up the fern-ace.

Why do pine trees love winter?
They can wear their fir coats.

What kind of tree likes doing housework?
A sweeping willow.

Why did the butterfly cry?
It saw the moth bawl.

What do you call a bee born in May?
A Maybe.

What insect can tell time?
A clockroach.

Which insects have the best manners?
Ladybugs.

Why shouldn't you tell secrets in a room full of beetles?
Because the room is bugged.

What do you call two beetle babies fighting over milk?
A beetle bottle battle.

How do gnats feed their young?
Gnaturally.

What's a flea's favorite plant?
A cattail.

What's a flea's second favorite plant?
  Dogwood.

Why don't ants smell?
  They wear deodor-ant.

What goes buzz, buzz, buzz, plop?
  A bee laughing its head off.

What do honeybees use to check out flowers?
  Bee-noculars.

Wacky Nature Books

How to Catch Butterflies by Annette N. Ajar

Collecting Clams and Mussels by Shelley Beech

How to Fetch a Pail of Water by Jack N. Jill

My Life as a Lumberjack by Tim Burr

Safe Winter Driving by I. C. Rhodes

Cross Country by Auto by Phil R. Upp

Crossing Streams by Carey Meover

Why Bees Love Flowers by Polly Nation

Strong Breezes by Gustav Wind

Making a Living in the Woods by Rob N. Hood

Why did the bee go south for the winter?
To visit an ant in Florida.

What do butterflies become after they graduate from college?
Mothematicians.

How do police get rid of mosquitoes?
They call out the SWAT team.

What do ants furnish their homes with?
Ant-iques.

Which bank does the sun go to?
Daylight Savings.

What did summer say to spring?
"Help! I'm going to fall!"

How can a hurricane see where it's going?
It has an eye in its middle.

What do riverbanks do their homework in?
Their notebrooks.

What flower do you get when you cross a violin
with a clarinet?
A violet.

Which flowers are happy to see you?
Glad-iolas.

If a buttercup is yellow, what color is a hiccup?
Burple.

Why did the hiker climb a mountain?
To get a peak at it.

Why don't mountains get cold in winter?
Because they wear snowcaps.

Why did Cinderella wish she had been magically turned into a tree?

She wanted to be very poplar.

Why did Mozart write his symphonies on a fallen tree?

He was de-composing.

Why did the silly boy take his piggy bank outdoors?

He heard there was going to be a change in the weather.

What should you do if you fall off your bicycle?

Get back on and re-cycle.

What falls on a mountain but never gets hurt?

Snow.

What did the mountain scream after the earthquake?

"It wasn't my fault!"

2. Animal Crackers

What kind of plane does an elephant fly?
A jumbo jet.

Why do grizzly bears live in caves?
Because they can't afford apartments.

How do reindeer kill insects?
With their ant-lers.

What do you call sheep that join law enforcement?
The Fleece Police.

What's a kangaroo's favorite year?
  Leap year.

Why do mother kangaroos hate rainy days?
  Because their kids want to play inside.

What do you call a crocodile that lives between two buildings?
  An alley-gator.

Why didn't the alligator finish its homework?
  It was swamped.

Are We There Yet?

What kind of cars do ponies drive?
Mustangs.

What kind of cars do hummingbirds drive?
Hum-vees.

What kind of cars do stinging insects drive?
Bee M. Ws.

What kind of cars do baby birds drive?
Hatchbacks.

What kind of cars do couch potatoes drive?
Convertibles.

What kind of cars do eels drive?
Electric ones.

What kind of cars do bakers drive?
Rolls.

What's a crocodile's favorite drink?
  Gatorade.

Where do rabbits get their food?
  At hopping centers.

Where do karate students get their food?
  At chopping centers.

What kind of crackers are bad for parrots?
  Firecrackers.

What do you call a lizard that wins the lottery?
  A chamelionaire.

What animal is smarter than a talking parrot?
  A spelling bee.

What kind of jokes do crows like?
  Corny ones.

What do you call a tiger in the snow?
  A cool cat.

What do you have to do before riding a horse
named Everest?
  Mount Everest.

What's a giraffe's favorite fruit?
  Neck-tarines.

What do skunks become after they take a bath?
  Ex-stinked.

What do seals wear with their bathrobes?
  Bedroom flippers.

What kind of cat rides in an ambulance?
  A first-aid kitten.

What happened when the cat ate a ball of yarn?
  She had mittens.

What's a cat's favorite TV show?
  The Evening Mews.

What do cats say when they want to go out-doors?
  "Me-out."

When is it bad luck to have a black cat following you?
  When you're a mouse.

How do mice revive each other?
  With mouse-to-mouse resuscitation.

What do mice use for bad breath?
  Mousewash.

How do chickens get into college?
  By passing their eggs-aminations.

How can you tell if there's an elephant in your sandwich?
  You need a crane to pick it up.

What would you get if a 50-ton duck stomped on the ground?
  An earthquack.

What kind of dogs do vampires own?
  Bloodhounds.

Where do dogs and cats buy their furniture?
  At flea markets.

What happened when the pelican flew over the
whale?
  It had a blast.

Wacky Animal Books

Why Cats Scratch by Manny Fleeze

Keep Your Pet Healthy by Ray B. Shott

How To Build a Better Mousetrap by Kit E. Katt

Why We Love Garbage Cans by Al E. and Tom Katt

Who Stole My Cheese? by Mick E. Mowce

Raising Bears at Home by Claude Updewall

Dogs Running Wild by Ty M. Upp

What do kangaroos ask for at motels?
 Kangarooms.

What's a cow's favorite movie?
  "The Sound of Moooosic."

What's a crayfish's favorite movie?
  "Fiddler Crab on the Roof."

What do whales use to hold their tails up?
  Blubber bands.

Why couldn't the baby whale use its blowhole?
  It was only a little squirt.

Why did the whale cross the ocean?
  To get to the other tide.

What's a ladybug's favorite singing group?
The Beetles.

Why don't crickets have antennae?
Because they get cable.

Where do spiders get their music?
Off the Web.

What kind of creatures rent videos?
Tapeworms.

What do you call a bird that flies into a telephone pole?
A black-and-bluejay.

What do you call a pig flying a helicopter?
A pork chopper.

What kind of spaceship do sheep fly?
Ewe F. Os.

3. People Pranksters

Why are pizza makers so wealthy?
  They're always rolling in dough.

Why would Snow White make a good judge?
  She's the fairest of them all.

What kind of car does Mickey Mouse drive?
  A Minnie van.

What should you do if a teacher rolls her eyes at you?
  Pick them up and roll them back to her.

Why did the lawyer take her iron to court?
She had pressing business.

What do you call a bunch of artists in a box?
A chest of drawers.

How did the lumberjack chop down a tree?
Axedentally.

What do sleepy gardeners use?
Yawn mowers.

C'mon In!

How do you welcome a skydiver?
"Glad you could drop in!"

How do you welcome a sailor?
"Nice to sea you."

How do you welcome Santa Claus?
"Make yourself at ho-ho-home."

How do you welcome a centipede?
"Put your feet, feet, feet, feet, feet, feet up."

How do you welcome an angel?
"Halo there, c'mon down!"

How do you welcome a grizzly bear?
"You're looking grrrrreat!"

What did the lamp say when the owner turned it off?
"Thanks a watt!"

Why did everyone laugh at the biologist?
He bent over and split his genes.

What do scientists do after they discover a new gene?
Cell-ebrate!

Why did the farmer plow his field with a steam-roller?
He wanted to grow mashed potatoes.

Wacky Library Books

I Can Do Anything by Will Power

How to Get Along With Your Sister
by Sharon Sharealike

Jewelry Collecting by Pearl Nicholas

Shakespeare's Phrases by Toby R. Nottaby

The Unfinished Story by Cliff Hanger

You Don't Say by Ida Claire

Why Amy Walked to School by Mr. Bus

Oops, I Did It Again! by Miss Take

Hopelessly Lost by Wes D. Eggzit

Embarrassed in the Shower by Kurt N. Fell

What does Farmer Darth Vader cultivate?
  His Force field.

How did the farmer mend his jeans?
  With a cabbage patch.

What do you call a chicken farmer?
  An eggspert.

Where do hogs live at the North Pole?
  In pigloos.

Why didn't your friend get the umbrella joke?
  It went right over her head.

What did the motorcyclists ask for at the motel?
A vroom-vrooom for two.

What do you call a princess with a tidy house?
Sweeping Beauty.

What did the driver say when she couldn't stop?
"Give me a brake!"

Why did the helicopter pilot quit the late shift?
It was a fly-by-night job.

Who invented a plane that couldn't fly?
The Wrong Brothers.

Why don't scuba divers make good grades?
  They're always below C-level.

What was the diver doing in his garage?
  Changing his shark plugs.

Why did the biologist stop feeding dolphins?
  She didn't see the porpoise in it.

Why did the two comic book characters fall in love?
  They were drawn together.

What do you get when a police officer surprises a skunk?

Law and odor.

How did the police officer know the suspects stole the ketchup?

He caught them red-handed.

What did the conductor say to the drummer?

"Beat it!"

How do carpenters greet each other?

"House it going?"

What did the contractor say when his electrician came to work at noon?
"Wire you insulate?"

Why are electricians so smart?
They keep up with current events.

What do you call a genius pig?
Einswine.

Why was Einstein's head wet?
He had a brainstorm.

What kind of scientist invented soda pop?
A fizzicist.

4. Silly Salad

What does an astronaut eat her spaghetti from?
  A satellite dish.

Why did the biscuit hurry to school?
  It didn't want to miss roll call.

Have you heard the peanut butter joke? I can't tell you—you might spread it around.

What do you get when you spill soda in a cornfield?
Popcorn.

How do you know when there's a turkey in your refrigerator?
All the food is gobbled up.

What animals like Mexican food?
Chili-con-carnivores.

What do penguins put in their salad?
Iceberg lettuce.

What do ship captains put on their salad?
Crew-tons.

What would you get if you dropped a French fry on the sofa?
A couch potato.

Where did the first bakery open?
On the yeast coast.

What should you do with rude pepperoni?
Give it a pizza your mind.

Who went to the Pizza Ball?
Cinderella Mozzarella.

How does Humpty Dumpty sunbathe?
Sunny-side up.

What do you call a funny book about eggs?
A yolk book.

What did Humpty Dumpty say to the comedian?
"You crack me up."

What channel are the dancing chocolate candies on?
M & MTV.

What's a spider's favorite picnic food?
Corn-on-the-cobweb.

How can you tell if a clock is hungry?
It goes back four seconds.

What kind of cake is served in a haunted house?
Eye scream cake.

What should you say to an unhappy cake?
"What's eating you?"

What kind of fruit do shellfish eat?
Crab apples.

What's a scarecrow's favorite fruit?
Strawberries.

What do quarterbacks like to do at dinner?
Pass the salt.

What kind of salt do gymnasts use?
Somersault.

What do you call fifteen-year-old salt?
A salt-teen.

What do you get when a waiter trips?
Flying saucers.

Where do vegetables volunteer?
The Peas Corp.

Where do bad vegetables go?
To the re-farm-atory.

What does a porcupine put on its submarine
sandwich?
Dill prickles.

Why are potatoes good detectives?
They always keep their eyes peeled.

What happened when the grape was promoted?
It got a raisin pay.

What's the best thing to take to the desert?
A thirst-aid kit.

What do alligators cook in?
Croc-pots.

Why do frogs have such an easy life?
Because they eat whatever bugs them.

Shut the Door . . . I'm Dressing!

What dressing does Popeye put on his salad?
  Olive Oyl.

What dressing do cowboys put on their salad?
  Ranch.

What dressing do sad people put on their salad?
  Blue Cheese.

What dressing do cruise directors put on their salad?
  Thousand Island.

What dressing does a Cyclops put on its salad?
  Screamy Eyetalian.

What dressing do nice cows put on their salad?
  Honey Moostard.

Who wears a red cape and leaps from restaurant roofs in a single bound?
Supperman.

Who has friends for lunch?
A cannibal.

What do horseflies do when you invite them to dinner?
They just drop in for a bite.

How do you save an elephant drowning in hot chocolate?
Throw in a marshmallow.

What did the teddy bear say when offered dessert?
"No, thanks, I'm stuffed."

What's a chimp's favorite ice cream?
Chunky Monkey.

What is a second scoop of ice cream called?
An ice cream clone.

How do giant sequoias like their ice cream served?
In pinecones.

What kind of fruit leaves holes in your tongue?
A porcupineapple.

Wacky Cookbooks

The Best Pizza Ever by Chris P. Krust

All About Peppers by Holly Peenyo

Microwave Leftovers by Luke Warmm

Outdoor Cooking by Barbie Q.

Snacks for a Crowd by Saul Ted P. Knotts

Cooking With Butter by Marge R. Inn

No More Coffee! by T. Baggs

Yummy Christmas Treats by Candy Kane

My Favorite Dessert by Dee Lishus

Healthy Vegetables by Artie Choke

Where do baby eagles eat?
  In high chairs.

Why did the silly student eat his homework?
  The teacher said it would be a piece of cake.

What would you get if potatoes took a bath?
  Soapspuds.

What did one plate say to the other plate?
  "Lunch is on me!"

5. Boo! Bloopers

Why do skeletons play piano?
  Because they don't have organs.

Where do skeletons live?
  On dead end streets.

Do mummies like being mummies?
  Of corpse!

What do ghosts wash their hair with?
  Shamboo.

What lies at the bottom of the ocean and twitches?
A nervous wreck.

How does a witch play loud music?
On her broom box.

What's a witch's favorite movie?
Star Warts.

What happens when a witch breaks the sound barrier?
You hear a sonic broom.

How do you welcome a ghost into your house?
  "Come right in and have a sheet."

What kind of construction vehicle does a ghost drive?
  A screamroller.

How do ghosts avoid computer eyestrain?
  They wear their spooktacles.

What do baby ghosts turn on before they go to bed?
  Their frightlights.

What do baby ghosts get when they fall down?
  Boo-boos.

Why couldn't the elf play outside with the other elves?
  He had too much gnomework.

Why was 6 afraid of 7?
  Because 7-8-9!

Who brings Christmas presents to werewolves?
  Santa Claws.

Why did the werewolf read *The Lord of the Rings* 50 times?
  It was hobbit-forming.

What do Egyptian mummies eat for lunch when they go to the beach?
Sand witches.

How do mummies hide?
They wear masking tape.

What kind of boats do vampires like?
Blood vessels.

How do little vampires get to sleep?
They count Draculas.

How does Dracula tell time?
He checks his clockroach.

Why can't Dracula play baseball?
He lost his bat.

Why doesn't Dracula like garlic?
It gives him bat breath.

What did the bat say to its girlfriend?
"You're fun to hang around with."

Who did Frankenstein take to the prom?
His ghoulfriend.

What do you call a haunted wasp?
A zom-bee.

Wacky Horror Books

Trade-In Body Parts by Frank N. Stein

Halloween Pumpkin Carving by Jack O.
 Lantern

How I Scared Goldilocks by Ted E. Bayer

Where Is Little Red Riding Hood?
 by I. M. DeWolf

UFOs Are Real! By A. Lee N. Bean

How to Dig a Grave by Barry D. Boddy

Night of the Werewolf by Harry Bakk

Tarantulas on the Loose by Isadore Open

I Died of Fright by Terry Fide

What happens when you take a picture of the Invisible Man?
Nothing develops.

What do you call a cloned kitten?
A mew-tant life form.

What does Tinkerbell ride at the amusement park?
The fairy-go-round.

How do you catch a fairy?
By its fairy tail.

How are spiders like ducks?
They both have webbed feet.

What would you get if two spiders wrestled?
Scrambled legs.

How big are centipedes?
One hundred feet long.

Where do you pay to use the Ogre Highway?
At the trollbooth.

6. Rap It Up, Please

Where do strawberries play their saxophones?
   At jam sessions.

What kind of music gets played at school?
   Class-ical.

Who plays country music at the beach?
   The fiddler crabs.

Where does a daffodil hear its favorite music?
   On a bloom box.

What did the Pied Piper say when he lost his flute?
"Oh, rats!"

Why couldn't Little Boy Blue blow his horn?
The sheep took it to band practice.

What part does a grizzly sing in the church choir?
Bearitone.

What do you call three oaks who sing together?
A tree-o.

Which orchestra leader has webbed feet?
The conducktor.

Band Aid

What instruments do doctors play in a band?
  Surgical ones.

What do surgeons play in a band?
  Organs.

What do turkeys play in a band?
  Drumsticks.

What do shoemakers play in a band?
  Soxophones.

What do skeletons play in a band?
  Trom-bones.

What do you call a dad who sings and dances?
  A Pop-star.

How is a movie like a broken leg?
  They both need a cast.

Why couldn't the piano go home after the concert?
It lost its keys.

What did the mother piano say to the baby grand?
"I don't like your tone, young man."

What do you get when you cross a BMW with a piano?
Car tunes.

What do pianists use to eat their steak?
Tuning forks.

Why was the pianist smacking her head on the keys?
She was playing by ear.

Why do baseball players make good pianists?
They have perfect pitch.

7. Mall Madness

When skunks go for groceries, where do they find the best bargains?

At shopping scenters.

Why don't bumblebees go shopping?

They're too buzz-y.

What happened to the origami shop that used to be on this block?

It folded.

Where do ghosts shop?

At boo-tiques.

Where do streams buy their novels?
At the brookstore.

How do grizzlies try on shoes?
Bearfoot.

What shoes should you buy when your basement is flooded?
Pumps.

What did the shoe say to the foot?
"You're putting me on!"

What kind of sneakers do birds buy?
Ones with vel-crow.

Where do sailors return damaged masts?
To the sails clerk.

How do hummingbirds stay dry?
They buy humbrellas.

What do you call a kangaroo clerk with bad manners?
Kangarude.

How do kangaroos add up their purchases?
With pocket calculators.

What kind of pens do skunks buy?
Ones with indelible stink.

Where would you buy 36 inches?
At a yard sale.

What does a house buy at the mall?
Address.

Where should you pay your car repair bill?
At the crash register.

What's an easy way to double your money?
Look at it in a mirror.

What do pigs buy for relaxing in the backyard?
Ham-mocks.

Wacky Shopping Books

Collecting Modern Paintings by Art X. Ibit

Fur, Fumes, and Flowers by Al R. Gee

Shopping on the Second Floor by Ellie Vader

Out of Breath at the Food Court by Noe S. Calator

Department Store Courtesy by May I. Helpyoo

The History of Footwear by Buck L. Myshoo

Shoplifting: A Serious Problem
   by Reed M. S. Wrights

Where do animals go when they lose their tails?
   To the retail store.

What did the duck say when she bought lipstick?
   "Please, just put it on my bill."

Why do department stores like cats?
They're pre-furred customers.

Did you hear about the two racing silkworms?
They ended up in a tie.

Why was the pajama store closed?
It's only open at nightie.

Which customers avoid early-bird sales?
  Worms.

What's the best time to shop for sporting goods?
  Ten-nish.

Why aren't gorillas allowed in furniture stores?
  They're always beating on their chests.

What happens to vacuum cleaners at a busy mall?
  They get pushed around.

Shop Till You Drop!

What do frogs buy at the mall?
Open-toad sandals.

What do clones buy at the mall?
Denim genes.

What do sheep buy at the mall?
Baaaath towels.

What do cats buy at the mall?
Purrfume.

What do bumblebees buy at the mall?
Bee-kinis.

What do chimney sweeps buy at the mall?
Sootcases.

What do mummies buy at the mall?
Wrapping paper.

How do billboards talk?
  In sign language.

How do leopards do their shopping?
  From cat-alogs.

Why did the bald man refuse to buy a wig?
  He didn't want toupee.

Why did the rabbit buy a house?
  It was tired of the hole thing.

Why did the rabbit get a job at the grocery store?
  It wanted a raise in celery.

8. Games & Groans

What's a baby's favorite ride?
A stroller coaster.

Why was Cinderella so bad at basketball?
Her coach was a pumpkin.

How does Mother Earth fish?
With north and south poles.

What do petunias wear when they exercise?
Sweatplants.

Why did the pecan work out?
It was a health nut.

How do locomotives work out?
With personal train-ers.

Where do trains work out?
At the track.

How do witches work out?
On hexercise machines.

How do bees start their exercises?
With swarm-ups.

Hit the Deck

What card game do construction workers play?
Bridge.

What card game do anglers play?
Go Fish.

What card game do nutty ice skaters play?
Crazy Eights.

What card game do cardiologists play?
Hearts.

What card game do prisoners play?
Solitaire.

What's a tornado's favorite game?
Twister.

What game do mice like to play?
Hide and squeak.

What's a baby sparrow's favorite game?
Beak-a-boo.

If Michael Jordan gets athlete's foot, what does Santa get?
Mistle toe.

What do you call wood that has nothing to play with?
Board.

Why would you bring a trampoline to a nightclub?
For the bouncers.

How do surfers greet each other?
With a tidal wave.

Get Going!

What do you say to a slow walnut?
"Get cracking!"

What do you say to a slow taxidermist?
"Do your stuff!"

What do you say to a slow pencil sharpener?
"Get to the point!"

What do you say to a slow pencil?
"Get the lead out!"

What do you say to a slow centipede?
"Shake a leg, leg, leg, leg, leg!"

What do you say to a slow rubber band?
"Make it snappy!"

What do waiters ask when playing tennis?
"May I serve?"

Why did the police go to the baseball stadium?
They heard someone was stealing bases.

What position do camels play on baseball teams?
Humpire.

Where should you sit at a ballpark if you want
your clothes to get really white?
In the bleachers.

Why don't grasshoppers go to lacrosse games?
They prefer cricket matches.

Who won the race between two balls of string?
They were tied.

What game do falcons play on ice?
Hawk-ey.

Why can't a *Tyrannosaurus rex* play hockey?
It keeps eating the goalie.

How do frogs protect their knees when skateboarding?
They wear lily pads.

How do pandas ride bikes safely?
They hold onto the handlebears.

How do rubber bands warm up?
They stretch.

What exercise does your nose do when you have a cold?
It runs.

What exercise do you do at church?
Knee bends.

Where do angels swing and slide?
At the prayground.

What did one dumbbell say to the other?
"Hey, weight for me!"

9. Open Wide!

How did the dentist fix the dragon's teeth?
  With a fire drill.

What does a donkey wear to straighten its teeth?
  Bray-ces.

Why did the oak tree see a dentist?
  To get a root canal.

What does a dentist tell in court?
"*The tooth, the whole tooth, and nothing but the tooth.*"

How did the snake like the doctor's joke?
It went into hiss-terics.

What did Mrs. Snake have at the hospital?
A bouncing baby boa.

Why do doctors measure snakes in inches?
Because snakes don't have feet.

How do you examine a sick tiger?
Give it a CAT scan.

What plant do you find in emergency rooms?
IV.

How do injured rubber bands get to the hospital?
On stretchers.

When do houses see a doctor?
When they have window panes.

Why did the basketball player go to the doctor?
He wanted to get more shots.

What do birds need when they're sick?
Tweetment.

When don't you feel so hot?
When you catch a cold.

How can you tell if a mummy has a cold?
He starts coffin.

How can you avoid getting a sharp pain in your eye when you drink chocolate milk?
Take the spoon out of the glass.

Where do dirty socks go when they get sick?
To the Detergency Room.

Wacky Medical Books

How to Heal a Sore Throat by Lauren Jitis

Medical Malpractice Suits by Sue M. Good

Shots Don't Hurt! by Ben Dover

How to Write a Prescription by Adeline Moore

Malaria Symptoms by Amos Quito

Veggies for Your Health by Brock O'Lee

Clone Yourself! by Gene Splitter

Everyday Dental Care by Pearl E. Teeth

How to Cure Stomach Pain by Tom E. Ake

What direction does a sneeze travel?
  Atchoo!

Where do cows buy their cough drops?
At the farm-acy.

Why did the cow go to the psychiatrist?
Because she was so mooooody.

Why can't a pony sing?
It's always a little horse.

Why did the fireplace call the doctor?
The chimney had the flue.

What sickness do rodeo riders get?
Bronc-itis.

Why did the germ cross the microscope?
To get to the other slide.

Why is an eye doctor like a teacher?
They both test the pupils.

What happens when an icicle falls on your head?
It knocks you cold.

What is a drill sergeant?
An army dentist.

What's the healthiest type of water?
Well water.

What's the perfect cure for dandruff?
Baldness.

What means of transportation gives people colds?
Achoo-choo train.

If an apple a day keeps the doctor away, what will an onion do?
Keep everyone away.

Why did the cookie go to the doctor?
It felt crumby.

Why should you tiptoe past the medicine cabinet?

So you won't wake the sleeping pills.

How did the clock feel when no one wound it up?

Run down.

What would you call a small wound?

A shortcut.

When do you have acute pain?

When you own a very pretty window.

If you don't feel well, what do you probably have?
Gloves on your hands.

What did Captain Hook do when he lost his hand?
He went to the second-hand shop.

If you dropped a tomato on your toe, would it hurt much?
Sure, if it were in a can.

What did Frankenstein say when a bolt of lightning hit him?
"Thanks, I needed that!"

10. Computer Chuckles

What should you do if you're stuck on the Web?
Call a spider.

What do you call flowers that use the Internet?
Smartyplants.

How do we know that spiders own computers?
They have their own websites.

What happens when the Wicked Queen turns on her computer?
The screen goes Snow White.

What did one keyboard say to the other keyboard?
  "You're not my type."

What should you do if your computer hums?
  Teach it the words.

What would you get if you kept typing antidisestablishmentarianism.com into your computer?
  Sore fingers.

What kind of chips are found in farmers' computers?
  Potato chips.

How do train conductors find information on the Internet?
  They use a search engine.

Weirdo Websites

Have you seen the leopard website?
No, I haven't spotted it yet.

Have you seen the hurricane website?
It really blew my mind!

Have you seen the goldfish website?
It really bowled me over!

Have you seen the fishing website?
It isn't online yet.

Have you seen the boxing website?
It knocked me out!

Have you seen the tomato website?
I'll ketchup with it later.

Have you seen the opticians' website?
It's a site for sore eyes.

Weirdo Websites

Have you seen the mountain website?
I must take a peak.

Have you seen the paper towel website?
It's very absorbing.

Have you seen the boomerang website?
You'll go back to it again and again.

Have you seen the garbage can website?
It's a load of rubbish.

Have you seen the adhesive tape website?
I can hardly tear myself away.

Have you seen the lions and tigers web-site?
I'm not wild about it.

Have you seen the alarm clock website?
It's very striking.

Why do beavers spend so much time on the Internet?
They never want to log off.

Where do snowmen put their websites?
On the Winternet.

Why did the computer sneeze?
It had a virus.

What should you do if you find a twig in your disk drive?
Speak to the branch manager.

What do you call a grandmother who designs programs?
A computer programma.

Wacky Computer Books

How to Clean Your Computer
   by Dusty Keebord

Let's All Ban Spam! by O. Kaye Bymee

How to Fix Spelling Mistakes by Dee Leete

The Greatest Online Story Ever Written!
   by Paige Turner

Set Up Your Own Website by Dot Comm

How to Get a High-Tech Job by Bea A. Nerd

The World's Largest Software Company
   by Mike Rosoft

How do teachers take attendance by
computer?
   They use scroll call.

What's a carpenter's favorite computer icon?
The toolbar.

What do computer programmers do on weekends?
Go for disk drives.

What would you get if you crossed a computer
with a ballerina?
The Netcracker Suite.

How can you learn ballet dancing on the Internet?
Use the tutu-torial.

Where does an elephant keep its laptop?
In its trunk.

What do you get if a tarantula sits on your computer?
A spider byte.

How does Old MacDonald send messages?
By e-i-e-i-o-mail.

Why don't you stamp e-mails?
Because your foot would go right through the screen.

How do Italian cooks swap recipes?
By spaghett-e-mail.

Why was the chicken banned from sending e-mails?
She was always using fowl language.

How do e-books communicate?
They page each other.

11. Crazy Celebrations

What did the rabbit buy his fiancée?
  A 14-carrot ring.

How do you keep a baby fly from crying?
  Give it a paciflyer.

What room should you take babies to when they cry?
  To the bawl room.

Why did Benny Bee get married?
He finally found his honey.

What do farmers give their wives when they marry?
Hogs and kisses.

What do maples give each other when they marry?
Tree rings.

What do hamburgers give each other when they marry?
Onion rings.

What did the pinky say to the thumb?
"I think I'm in glove with you."

What happens when two angels get married?
They live harpily ever after.

Who gets married at a witch's wedding?
The bride and broom.

What do you call two married spiders?
Newly-webs.

What does a duck wear to a wedding?
A duxedo.

Who do pelicans bring with them to weddings?
Their gullfriends.

How did the mushrooms like the reception?
They had a lot of fun-gi.

What does Hamlet eat on his birthday?
Danish.

What do squirrels eat on their birthdays?
Donuts.

What should you do if your birthday cake tastes crunchy?
Spit out the plate.

Cut the Cake!

What do mice eat on their birthdays?
Cheesecake.

What do rabbits eat on their birthdays?
Carrot cake.

What do demons eat on their birthdays?
Devil's food cake.

What do saints eat on their birthdays?
Angel food cake.

What do dwarfs eat on their birthdays?
Shortcake.

What do divers eat on their birthdays?
Sponge cake.

What do grouchy cows eat on their birthdays?
Sour cream cake.

What do carpenters eat on their birthdays?
Pound cake.

What do police eat on their birthdays?
Cop cakes.

What does an oyster do on its birthday?
Shellabrate.

What do you always get on your birthday?
One year older.

When do kangaroos celebrate their birthdays?
In leap years.

What birthday game do cows play?
Mooooosical chairs.

Why didn't the skeleton go to the birthday party?
It had no body to go with.

Why can't monkeys send birthday presents?
The stamps keep sliding off the bananas.

What do you sing before a robin blows out its candles?

"Happy Bird-day to You!"

What do you sing when the letter U has a birthday?

"Happy Birthday to U!"

Who should you call if you have 100 candles on your cake?

The fire department.

Why do you put candles on top of a birthday cake?

Because you can't light them if you put them on the bottom.

What's the best thing to put into your Easter basket?

Your hand.

What does Santa eat first out of his Easter basket?

Belly beans.

What do tarantulas drink on Halloween?

Apple spider.

What do turkeys dress up as for Halloween?

Gobblins.

What do canaries do on Halloween?

Trick or tweet!

Prom Night

How did Molly Mare wear her hair to the prom?
In a ponytail.

How did Brenda Baker wear her hair to the prom?
In a bun.

How did Sarah Sow wear her hair to the prom?
In pigtails.

How did Colleen Contortionist wear her hair to the prom?
In a twist.

How did Benny Bee wear his hair to the prom?
In a buzz cut.

Wacky Celebration Books

Some Day My Prince Will Come
by Crystal Slippers

How To Plan A Fun Party by Will I. C. U.
Thayer

My Favorite Easter Gift by Pat A. Bunnee

Too Excited to Sleep! by Eliza Wake

365 Simple Celebrations by Anita Dayoff

How I Became a Millionaire by Nick L. N.
Dyme

The Secrets to a Long Life by Vera Olde

Belated Birthdays by M. T. Handed

Holidays from A to Z by Dick Shenary and
Alfie Bett

Why did the silly guest take a bowl of salsa with him when he went swimming?
His host said, "Please take a dip in my pool."

What kind of parties do bricklayers attend?
Cement mixers.

Did you hear about the party in the basement?
It made the Best Cellar List.

What does a werewolf say when the party's over?
"Fangs a lot for inviting me!"

Index